Llanerchaeron

Ceredigion

YR YMDDIRIEDOLAETH GENEDLAETHOL
THE NATIONAL TRUST

ELEGANCE AND TRADITION

1   2   3   4

CRADLED in the wooded valley of the River Aeron lies a traditional rural estate that has been in the same family for ten generations. Over three centuries, each generation has added something to Llanerchaeron. Today, it is still all here – house, servants' quarters, stables, farm buildings and walled garden, set in a landscape which is both beautiful and productive. Of the many people who helped to create and cherish this place, four are central to the story.

1 Colonel William Lewis (d.1828)

Soon after Lewis inherited the estate in 1789, he commissioned a new house from John Nash, who had already worked for his cousins. It was completed about 1795. Lewis was a man of great energy and vision, pioneering modern agricultural methods on the estate and helping to develop Aberaeron and Aberystwyth.

2 Mary Ashby Lewis (1813–1917)

In 1841, at the age of 28, she married Colonel Lewis's only son, John William, who had inherited Llanerchaeron in 1828. John William Lewis reroofed the house, added a bay window to the Morning Room, and built the free-standing Billiard Room in 1845, but did little else to the property before he died in 1855. She found herself running the estate single-handedly and did not die until 1917, aged 104, having been at Llanerchaeron for over three quarters of a century.

3 Captain Thomas Powell Lewes (1860–1940)

John William Lewis's great-nephew, T.P. Lewes, introduced electricity and modern plumbing, but continued to run the house in the old style throughout the 1920s and '30s. He loved walking and country sports, keeping his own pack of fox and otter hounds.

4 John Powell Ponsonby Lewes (1900–89)

Known as Ponsonby Lewes, he inherited his father's passion for hunting. He was a quiet man, who continued the traditions of his family. On his death he bequeathed the estate to the Trust.

Left Nash's villa at Llanerchaeron lies at the heart of the wooded Aeron valley

The Nash villa

Llanerchaeron is a remarkably unaltered, early work by the great Regency architect, John Nash. In 1783, at the age of 31, Nash had gone bankrupt. He retreated from London to Wales to rebuild his reputation, designing several villas like Llanerchaeron for the Welsh gentry. Career restored, he went on to conceive the Brighton Pavilion and Buckingham Palace for George IV.

At first sight, the house is simplicity itself – a plain two-storey box of stucco and slate. But Nash placed it with great care to make the most of the views across the Picturesque landscape. He arranged the principal rooms around a central, top-lit staircase hall. The interiors show his mastery of complex shapes and subtle classical detail. Look out especially for the plasterwork friezes: no two are the same, and all are of the highest quality. The extensive service quarters were placed out of sight at the back of the house.

A self-sufficient estate

At Llanerchaeron, you can discover a way of life that has almost entirely vanished in Wales. In the late 18th century, the estate was in the forefront of local agriculture, with the latest farm buildings. Llanerchaeron could supply all its own needs, but was also very much part of the local community. In the 20th century, hunting and fishing were central to life on the estate.

The P.M. Ward Bequest

In 1994 Miss P.M. Ward bequeathed her personal collection of artefacts to the National Trust, together with a substantial endowment. Although the collection has no particular connection with Llanerchaeron, it brings a fascinating extra interest to any visit. And it was only thanks to Miss Ward's generosity that the National Trust could afford to restore the estate to good health, and ensure its long-term future.

Top A cigarette packet, glass bottle and other items found under the floorboards during restoration

Above Glass decanter stoppers and shoe buckles from the P.M. Ward Bequest, changing displays of which are presented at Llanerchaeron

Right Nash's villa

Llanerchaeron represents
the result of ten generations'
sensitive management.
Working in harmony with
this tradition, the National
Trust continues to farm
the estate organically.
This will help to maintain
Llanerchaeron's rich diversity
of habitats and species,
and the beauty of the place.
The Trust also intends to
make the estate a showplace
for new and old techniques
of conservation.

Above Fitting a new beam
in the stock sheds

Left This elegant window
to the Dining Room is in
fact false – inserted by Nash
purely for the sake of
symmetry

TOUR OF THE HOUSE

THE ENTRANCE HALL is dominated by an extensive display of taxidermy, notably fox and otter masks and several unusual specimens, including an albino pheasant. Hunting took place regularly on the estate and elsewhere in the locality, and only finally ceased in 1968.

The hall chairs bearing the arms of the Lewes family – an eagle with a snake in its beak – are from Llysnewydd, another local house designed by Nash about 1795 for William Lewes, the great-great-grandfather of Ponsonby Lewes. The house at Llysnewydd was demolished in 1971.

Nash created an elegantly proportioned space, with an emphasis on simplicity through the use of relatively plain, but finely detailed, plasterwork.

He planned it as two distinct spaces, set at right-angles and hidden from each other, so that visitors entering the Inner Hall would be surprised by the sight of the double cantilevered staircase, with daylight flooding it from an unknown source.

The recent redecoration of the Hall with dusky pink-stone walls and blue-green balustrade is based upon paint analysis and research, and re-creates the first decorative scheme of the 1790s.

Above The Doric porch

Left The Entrance Hall

Right The main staircase

Far right Cases of taxidermy in the Entrance Hall

The Dining Room

The room retains Nash's original plan, with windows facing south over the park. Later alterations include a Victorian marble chimney-piece with 20th-century grate, a picture rail, Lincrusta paper below the dado rail, and wood graining of the originally pale-coloured joinery. The floor was also finished with chocolate brown varnish – a treatment repeated throughout the house. This redecoration was probably undertaken by Captain T.P. Lewes during his modernisation of the house after 1918. To complete the scheme, a reproduction of the original early 20th-century mica print ceiling paper has been hung.

This room is also dominated by the theme of hunting and contains further cases of taxidermy, including the first woodcock shot by T.P. Lewes, on 7 January 1874, when he was fourteen years old, and another shot by Ponsonby Lewes in 1911, when he was eleven.

The portrait in oils is of Colonel John Lewis, by John Walton. The 1890 coloured engraving of *A Foxhunter's Dream* was taken from a painting by A.C. Havell.

Two of the silver cups on the buffet were won by Captain T.P. Lewes's beagles at the Carmarthen Dog Show in 1872 and 1873. The large portrait photograph is of William Price Lewes, Ponsonby Lewes's grandfather.

The dining-table was manufactured by Henry Ogden of Manchester and, together with the dining-chairs, was probably brought here in the 1920s by Captain and Mrs Lewes. The rise-and-fall light over the dining-table is very similar to those supplied by Gillows and other manufacturers in the 1920s.

Masters of Hounds.

1885 & 6.

Wⁿ. Hʏ. Tᴜᴄᴋ, Aʀᴛɪꜱᴛ. (ᴄᴏᴘʏʀɪɢʜᴛ) 32, Sᴛ. Jᴀᴍᴇꜱ'ꜱ Sᴛ. Lᴏɴᴅᴏɴ, S.W.

Top 'My First Woodcock'. Shot by T.P. Lewes on 7 January 1874, when he was fourteen

Above The Dining Room dado is decorated with embossed 'Lincrusta' wallpaper

Left Masters of Hounds, 1885–6

Far left The Dining Room

LOOKING UP

If you look up in any of the main rooms at where the wall meets the ceiling, you will see a plasterwork frieze. Nothing unusual in that. But at Llanerchaeron, Nash took immense care in designing these decorative mouldings: in the Drawing Room, for instance, they feature narrow beading, acanthus leaves and flowers within twisted 'guilloche' patterns.

Right A Wedgwood blue plaque from one of the ebonised cabinets in the Drawing Room

The Drawing Room

The principal reception room of the house was skilfully orientated to provide a picturesque view across the park to St Non's church, which was remodelled in 1798 (although altered further in the late 19th century). The room was changed in the 1920s, but has recently been restored to Nash's original plan: the marble chimneypiece reinstalled on the south, elliptical wall, and the cupboard on the east wall re-created to reflect the symmetry of Nash's original design.

The early 20th-century decorative scheme of a buff-coloured and mica striped wallpaper and a mica print ceiling paper has been copied, and redecoration work has been carried out.

The room is dominated by a suite of ebonised cabinets with blue Wedgwood plaques and seat furniture (originally upholstered in an ochre-coloured wool known as 'rep') supplied by Thomas Turner, a cabinetmaker active in Manchester during the 1870s–90s. It may have

originally have been bought by T.P. Lewes's wife, Annie, who came from Wilmslow near Manchester.

The oval pastel portrait in the elaborate gold frame is of Colonel William Lewis, who commissioned the house from John Nash in the 1790s. It is an early work by Thomas Lawrence.

The watercolour portraits in oval frames are of Captain and Mrs Lewes's children: Ponsonby, aged three, who was later to bequeath Llanerchaeron to the National Trust, and his elder sister Gwladys, aged four. The pair of portrait photographs is of Colonel William and Ann Lewes, grandparents of Ponsonby Lewes. The oval portrait photograph is of T.P Lewes's father-in-law. Other pictures include three seascapes by D.G. Munro Hughes of the 1890s.

The silver inkstand was presented to Colonel William Price Lewes in July 1881 by the Royal Carmarthen Artillery Militia on his retirement after 22 years as its commander.

Above Ponsonby Lewes, aged three

Left *Sheep and Lambs*, 1876, by Eugène Verboeckhoven, the greatest Belgian animal painter of the 19th century

The Library

Once part of the earlier, mid-17th-century house, which Nash incorporated into his villa, the room has smaller proportions, including a lower ceiling and surviving earlier joinery details. Nash inserted a door in the north-west corner to provide access to the pleasure grounds and the service courtyard. The room includes elements from the 1920s as well as later 20th-century additions, such as the fireplace. The room has recently been redecorated, but re-creates almost exactly its appearance during the latter part of Ponsonby Lewes's lifetime, when it was his principal sitting room and study.

The original books, described in the 1918 sale catalogue as 'about 1000 volumes including well-bound books of Swift, Scott and Byron', were all sold, presumably along with the earlier bookcases. The present Library has a handful of early books: *The Works of the Famous Nicholas Machiavel* was printed in 1675. But the majority reflect the interests of the family, with a large number devoted to hunting. These include practical manuals and reference books as well

as quantities of Victorian fiction of the 1880s, much of it belonging to Annie Lewes.

The witty hunting prints are taken from a series depicting *The Adventures of Professor Muddle* by Finch Martin. The photograph depicts Captain T.P. Lewes with the hunt.

The Morning Room

Facing east to enjoy the best of the morning sunlight, this room also formed part of the earlier building on the site. In the mid-19th century, a bay window was inserted which disturbed the symmetry of the exterior façade. In 1996 the National Trust replaced it with a copy of the original 18th-century window. The room was also remodelled in the 1920s, when an additional door on the fireplace wall that led down steps into the cellar was blocked. A more efficient modern grate and a picture rail were also added, and the joinery was wood-grained.

The corner cabinet is from the suite now in the Drawing Room. The chairs are upholstered in a 'Jazz Age' cut cotton-velvet, originally coloured salmon and brown and typical of the 1930s.

The photographs are of Captain T.P. Lewes, one of his three sisters, and, on the cabinet, his daughter Gwladys.

Walk up the first flight of stairs and take the right-hand flight to the first floor

Above **The Reed Player**. An 'art study' by W. & D. Downey, inspired by the Victorian classical paintings of Lord Leighton

Right **The Library**

Above right **The Adventures of Professor Muddle**, by Finch Martin

Far right **The Morning Room**

Above The firescreen in the
Boudoir is decorated with
sepia photographs of actors
and other celebrities of the
late 19th century

Right The top-floor landing

The Landing

Nash skilfully concealed the differing floor levels of the old and new house by adding three further steps to link the landing and a top-lit lobby. Beneath the glazed conical roof-light, five symmetrically placed doors open into the principal bedrooms and dressing rooms.

A further roof light over the main stairs was installed by Captain T.P. Lewes in the 1920s to bring more light onto the stairs. This, however, entailed removing three servants' bedrooms on the attic floor.

The elaborate brass brackets, dating from the 1860s, originally supported oil lamps, which were superseded in 1919, when direct current electricity was installed.

On the top landing take the first door on the left

The Boudoir

Intended as a private sitting room for the women of the house, this was later known as the sewing room. The plasterwork is the most decorative and feminine in the house and includes a ceiling rose modelled in the form of radiating peacock feathers surrounded by garlands of wheat husks. At cornice level, rope mouldings are entwined with leaves. As in the Dressing Room on the opposite side of the landing, Nash incorporated a bowed door and an apse in each corner, into one of which the cupboard was inserted in the 1920s.

The mahogany cupboard survives from the early 19th century. Miss Biffin, a disabled artist who worked with a brush in her mouth, painted the watercolour above the fireplace of *The Marchioness of Abercorn at the Cottage of Industry*. The picture was sold in 1868 from the collection of Thomas Whiteley and probably brought to the house by Captain and Mrs Lewes. Other small items include her silver glasses case and, on the japanned shelves, a photograph in an ivory frame of Ponsonby Lewes as a small boy.

Below A curved door opens into the oval Boudoir

Captain Lewes's Bedroom and Dressing Room

The Bedroom was remodelled in the 1920s, when the fitted wardrobe and chimneypiece were installed. The bedroom suite in light ash of about the 1870s was probably brought here by Captain and Mrs Lewes. Photographs on the dressing table include Ponsonby Lewes as a boy fishing and driving his car. The oil portrait is of his son Derrick Lewes. The other oil, *Hastings from East Hill*, is by W.H. Burrow.

The adjoining Dressing Room is slightly less elaborate than Mrs Lewes's Dressing Room. It retains its late 18th-century Carrara marble chimneypiece and iron grate and Nash's finely detailed plasterwork.

The carpet is *en suite* with one in the adjacent Bedroom and is a particularly good example of a machine-made Axminster, the design and colouring of which echo the work of the Art Nouveau designer Charles Rennie Mackintosh.

This room and the adjacent bedroom are hung with their original lace sun curtains. It is extremely rare for such fragile textiles to survive: those elsewhere in the house are modern replicas of 1900s–1920s designs.

Mrs Lewes's Bedroom and Dressing Room

The principal bedroom was modernised by Captain Lewes in the 1920s, when the original chimneypiece was replaced and a fitted wardrobe installed. During the recent restoration, all the plasterwork in the house was cleaned and repaired. In this room conservators worked for many weeks to uncover the original design of flower heads which had been completely obliterated by a later layer of plaster.

The machine-made Axminster carpet matches that in the adjacent Dressing Room, and was probably supplied during the 1920s redecoration.

Above Anticipation, 1896 (Captain Lewes's Dressing Room)

Right Mrs Lewes's Bedroom

The watercolour portrait is of Ponsonby Lewes as a young boy. Other photographs of his son Derrick and his maternal grandmother are on the furniture.

The dressing room attached to Mrs Lewes's Bedroom is one of the finest rooms in the house, but, perhaps surprisingly, it is also the most private. It is gracefully shaped, with curved east and west walls, a bowed door and a niche in each corner, as well as a shallow coved ceiling. Its elegance arises from the architecture rather than the plasterwork, which is highly restrained. As in the Drawing Room, Nash carefully considered the views out of the house, in this case towards St Non's church.

The mahogany washstand and chest of drawers were specially designed for the room and are among a few original furnishings not to have been removed in 1918. The watercolours by V. Pozzi Drey are dated 1876. They were framed in Manchester and therefore probably brought to the house by Captain and Mrs Lewes.

Go back down the stairs to the landing and take the first door on the left

THE AXMINSTER CARPETS in Captain Lewes's Bedroom and Dressing Room were probably laid in the 1920s and have survived in remarkably good condition. The pattern recalls the Art Nouveau style of the Scottish designer Charles Rennie Macintosh.

Left Mrs Lewes's Dressing Room

Above and right Pamela
Ward in print and paint

The P.M. Ward Collection

In 1994 the National Trust was bequeathed a remarkable collection of artefacts by Miss P.M. Ward, along with a generous endowment. Her will stipulated that the collection was to be housed in a Georgian house, and her Trustees agreed that it should come to Llanerchaeron.

Born in 1908, Miss Ward spent her early years in India before returning to live in Eastbourne. She also travelled extensively in Europe and finally established an antique shop in London. Miss Ward's ashes are interred in St Non's churchyard.

The collection is an amalgamation of Miss Ward's personal collection and the stock from her Kensington shop, much of it carefully labelled with her own notes and price tickets. Miss Ward had a strong eye for design, and all the objects, largely household items or objects associated with pastimes, have a highly decorative quality. These have been arranged in her original cabinets in two former bedrooms. The scale of the collection enables the National Trust to change the displays periodically. Further details about the contents of each case can be obtained from the Room Steward.

Turn right and right again into the Servants' Corridor

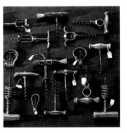

Top Fans and decorated boxes

Above Corkscrews

Left Children's games

19

IN THE 18TH CENTURY, this area was originally used by both family and visitors and includes what may have been the Nursery. From the later 19th century it was used by servants. On the wall on the left are a number of photographs illustrating the family's interest in hunting, including scenes from an otter hunt on the river Aeron.

A Servant's Bedroom

This small bedroom was probably intended for use by a nurserymaid: the nursery was situated close by. The room with its simple fireplace and grate retains a large area of 19th-century striped and sprigged wallpaper. As one of the only wallpapers dating from this period to survive in the house, it was conserved during the recent restoration.

Continue to the end of the corridor and go all the way down the stairs. At the bottom, turn left to go down to the cellars

The Cellars

Constructed of stone and consisting of three barrel-vaulted rooms, the cellars formed part of the 17th-century house on the site. Nash installed steps leading down from the Bell Corridor. In the west cellar original brackets and stands survive for the beer barrels, as does the ladder used for bringing barrels down into the cellar. The tap on the far wall may have delivered beer direct from the Brew-house, as was common practice, allowing it to be cooled on the way and the barrels filled *in situ*, although to date no pipework has been discovered leading underground from the Brew-house. The east cellar was used for storing wine and was also accessible from the Morning Room above, until the connecting door was blocked in the 1920s.

Go back up the steps to the Bell Corridor

The Bell Corridor

The service rooms were conveniently arranged at ground-floor, rather than basement, level, along a spinal corridor leading in logical order from the Butler's Pantry near the summoning bells to the Scullery and Kitchen, and then on to the Service Courtyard.

Turn left into the Butler's Pantry

Above The 19th-century wallpaper in the Servant's Bedroom

Right The Servant's Bedroom

Left The Beer Cellar

The Butler's Pantry

The Butler, as the most senior member of the staff, required prompt access to the family and thus to the mechanical, and later electric, bell boards, which were clearly visible to him through the small window overlooking the Bell Corridor. From here he was able to monitor servants going up and down the back stairs. He also had responsibility for the wines and so was conveniently close to the cellar.

Between 1861 and 1891 five different butlers served Mary Ashby Lewis: Samuel Halton, who came from Wigan, Lancashire, was paid £50 a year – a generous allowance when compared to that of Sarah Jones, a laundrymaid, who served the family for three decades for an annual salary of £11.

The cupboards, installed in the 19th century, would have been used to store the 'Silver and old Sheffield plate' listed in the 1918 sale catalogue. Valuable glass would have been washed up in a lead-lined sink, later replaced by the ceramic sink. The room was both practical and comfortable, and would also have been used as the Butler's private sitting room. Although almost no original contents survive from this room, furnishings have been added from elsewhere.

Return to and walk down the Bell Corridor, which also housed the Housekeeper's Room and Housemaids' Sitting Room. Turn right at the far end and right again into the Kitchen

The Kitchen

The Kitchen was designed by Nash to provide a well-lit and ventilated room, with plenty of storage space on the large dresser for the copper ware and other kitchen equipment, all of which was sold in 1918. There were a large 19th-century closed range at the southern end (replaced by the solid fuel Esse in the 20th century) and, in the arched recess on the north wall, a stewing stove heated by charcoal. The latter is a replica of that installed about 1800.

Like the Butler's Pantry, few original contents survive, but the Kitchen, Scullery and Larder are furnished with loans from Ceredigion Museum, gifts and loans from private individuals, and objects from the Geler Jones Collection.

The bracket on the right-hand side of the door dates from the 1890s and was used to support a set of 'Kenrick' scales.

Walk straight ahead into the Scullery

The Scullery and Larder

The Scullery was used for preparing food, especially meat and vegetables, and washing dishes. Cream and cheese produced in the nearby Dairy, and vegetables grown in the Walled Garden would have been delivered to the back door. The restored copper boiler, with its firebox and ashpit, provided hot water for the Kitchen, and, before the bathroom was installed, also for the family, to whose bedrooms it was carried up in large metal cans. The closed stove of the 1880s was recently installed in the location of the 19th-century original.

The Larder was added sometime before 1889. Here provisions would have been stored for use in the Kitchen and Scullery. Gauze, rather than glass, in the windows ensured that the room was kept cool and well ventilated.

Exit through the backdoor into the Service Courtyard where you may wander freely

ON THE MENU
The cooks, who were all
either English or Scottish,
had access to a wide range
of fresh produce. Veal, beef,
mutton, pork and chicken
were all provided by the
Home Farm, as well as a
variety of game (much of
it shot by members of the
family). Also available were
freshwater fish from the
Aeron and sea fish brought
into the harbour at
Aberaeron.

Left **The Scullery**

23

THIS IS ONE of the most fascinating and important areas of Llanerchaeron and it is almost unique in surviving in its original form. Planned for maximum efficiency, it included overhanging eaves to protect the servants walking between the rooms from the weather. Herringbone-patterned pitching using pebbles gathered from the nearby beach also provided a practical surface in the centre of the yard.

In many other houses, the late 18th-century fittings were superseded by later technology, but the majority survive here. The three ranges contain all that was required to run the house and estate as a model country villa.

To the left, the west range includes the *Dairy* with its large solid slate cream pans. An adjacent *Dairy Scullery* contains a hob grate to heat water for washing and scalding. The *Cheese Press Room* has its original presses, and on the other side is a *Cheese Store* for maturing the cheeses. The north wing, not originally part of Nash's scheme for the courtyard, was added by the 1840s. It includes a combined *Bake-house and Smoke-house*, the oven for which was modified in the 19th century, when a new brick oven was built in front of the original. The adjacent *Salting Room* contains slate tables and lead-lined tanks, where fresh meat was preserved with salt and brine, and a *Brew-house*, where 'small' beer, drunk instead of water, was made on a weekly basis. The east range houses a *Dry Laundry* with an Edwardian laundry stove. Here damp clothes were pressed and then hung on large drying racks to air. The washing itself was carried out in a small wet laundry by the river, where the drying ground was also sited. Other rooms provided storage, and the first-floor rooms were used as *Servants' Bedrooms*.

Leave the Service Courtyard through the arched corridor and go to the stone building ahead and to your right

The Billiard Room

This was built in 1843 by the estate mason David Morgan as a games room for John William Lewis. Erected at a time when billiards was becoming an increasingly popular game, it was, unusually, sited separately from the main house. An Aberystwyth-based architect, William Ritson Coultart, who was paid a fee of £20 in 1845, probably designed it. The clerestory windows allowed an even light to fall on the billiard table. The family and their male guests would have reached it from the villa via a door from the Library, as it would have been quite inappropriate for them to have walked through the service wing to reach the building.

The room now houses an exhibition about Llanerchaeron and the Trust's work on the estate.

Turn left out of the Billiard Room and follow signs to the Walled Garden

Top **The Service Courtyard**

Above **The Dairy**

Right **The Billiard Room** is housed in a separate building behind the Service Courtyard

Left **The Cheese Press Room**

THE WALLED GARDEN

A PRODUCTIVE kitchen garden was an important feature of any self-sufficient estate. The garden consists of two brick-walled enclosures, each about an acre in size. The walls were built at the end of the 18th century (at the same time as the villa) and in the west garden are constructed entirely of hand-made bricks using clay dug from a nearby field, 'Cae Pwll', which were then fired in another field, 'Cae Bricks'.

Orientated so that the longest walls face south, each garden is divided into plots (so that crops could be rotated), and surrounded by box-edged paths. Parts of the walls were heated by a system of hot-air flues fed by brick fire pits built on their north side. Protective covers or glass frames were often fixed to these 'hot walls' so that tender fruit could be grown.

The remains of an early 19th-century glasshouse with two central beds survive in the west garden. Warmed by fermenting horse dung or tanning bark, these 'hot beds' were used to force early crops and cultivate pineapples, melons and cucumbers.

Further glasshouses were added by the 1880s: the remains of one can be seen under the 1950s concrete greenhouse. The other glasshouses include a mid-19th-century Fernery and a Boulton & Paul greenhouse dating from after 1875. Between the two a Vinery was inserted, and the whole heated by a system of hot-water pipes, dating from about the 1880s.

In 1863 the *Bailiff's House*, overlooking the Walled Garden, garden yard and farm, was built for Thomas Baynton and his family. Thomas worked at Llanerchaeron for 40 years, overseeing activities in the garden and on the farm for Mary Ashby Lewis. By the 1920s Captain T.P. Lewes was employing four full-time gardeners. Although numbers declined following his death, the gardens

were still in full production in the 1940s: tomatoes, grapes and rhubarb, as well as plants, were sold locally. The garden is now cultivated with the support of many enthusiastic volunteers and still produces fruit and vegetables, which are often available for sale.

Leave the Walled Garden by the door leading from the north side of the east garden and enter the Rickyard, part of the Home Farm

Above The onion beds

Above right An espaliered apple tree in blossom

Right Herbs in the eastern section of the Walled Garden

Left Harvesting squashes and onions in the Walled Garden

The Rickyard

The yard is bounded on the left by the Threshing Barn, and to the right lie five late 18th-century rick stands. Three were used for stacking hay and two for sheaves of wheat or barley, keeping them off wet ground until ready for threshing on the floor of the nearby Threshing Barn. The cross-headed gaps provided ventilation to prevent the stacks overheating.

The Threshing Barn

One of the oldest buildings within the Home Farm, the barn was used to process and store cereals grown on the estate. Below the eaves, a series of square openings in the stonework are nesting boxes for pigeons, the birds providing a useful source of eggs and meat in the 18th century. The building is divided into two sections, each with its own timber threshing floor. The four pairs of large doors (two pairs face the Stockyard) provided access for loaded farm vehicles and generated a cross-draught to help separate wheat from chaff during the threshing process.

*Walk straight ahead between the Threshing Barn to the left and the **Pole Barn** on the right and in front of the **Saw Pit Shed**. Turn left and left again into the **Stockyard**, passing the **Carpenter's Workshop** and the **Gun Shed** on the left*

The Stockyard and Kennels

The yard and open-fronted stock sheds housed cattle in the winter and are still used for cows and calves. At the west end the *Boiler-house* contains both a firepit and 19th-century boiler used to heat the three glasshouses on the other side of the wall. The raised pitched paths in front of the sheds and the pigsties provide a drained and dry surface in an otherwise mucky yard. Manure gathered here was spread on the outlying fields. On the north side of the yard is a set of mid-19th-century pigsties; the pork was cured in the Smoke-house and Salting Room. At the western end, the *Mash Shed* was used to boil up mash for the pigs, the working and carriage horses, and, later on, the hounds. At the opposite end, another boiler heated up pig-swill, and, later, meat for the hounds.

The pigsties were later used as kennels for nearly 40 of Captain T.P. and Ponsonby Lewes's otter and fox hounds, as well as retrievers, terriers and ferrets. Two of the original dog benches survive, which were used until the 1970s.

Walk back out of the yard and turn left past the Granary. Walk up the steps to see the first floor

Below **The Rickyard with the Threshing Barn beyond**

Left Keith Jones the estate carpenter

THE HEAVY HORSE STABLE

The Stable was used for working horses and still retains its early 19th-century stalls, mangers and racks. The stalls are quite short and may have been designed for Welsh cobs, a sturdy and powerful breed used for ploughing and other farm work. Opposite the stable is a wooden rack originally used to air the leather horse collars after a hot day's work.

Right A leather horse collar in the Heavy Horse Stable

The Granary

The upper floor of the Granary contains a series of timber bins in which grain was stored. The room was kept ventilated by the louvered openings on all sides except the west, where the prevailing winds would have driven in the rain. An access hatch in the floor allowed grain to be shovelled directly onto a cart below. Sacks of grain could also be hauled up by pulley. The open ground floor, with open bays and stone piers (designed to support the full grain bins), was used for storing farm carts.

Continue left past the Granary and turn left past the Heavy Horse Stable and Cowshed

The Cowshed

The 18th-century Cowshed was originally a stand-alone byre, before the Bailiff's House and the Heavy Horse Stable were added. It was later converted into a milking parlour, and many of the original doors were blocked. The milking machinery was used until the 1970s.

Return past the Heavy Horse Stable and turn left into the Garden Yard

The Garden and Frame Yards

They contain the Potting Shed, which was an essential store and working area still used by the gardeners. It contains two firepits whose flues heated the garden walls on their south side. The Frame Yard contains two frames heated by hot-air flues, the furnace for which is behind the restored frame. The steps leading up behind the frame provided access to the Fruit Store, where orchard fruit was carefully laid out on wooden racks to provide the family with fresh fruit during the winter.

Leave the Garden Yard and turn left into the Carriage and Stable Courtyard

The Carriage and Stable Courtyard

Dating from about 1800, the yard consists of three different ranges, which were created from several smaller buildings integrated to form a courtyard, complete with *trompe-l'oeil* windows on the two north-facing gables and a herringbone-pitched yard. Although functional, it was designed to have a formal and decorative appearance, since the family and their guests would have made visits to view the horses.

The east range consists of a set of stables complete with surviving stalls, mangers and a tack room. The carriage and riding horses were stabled here. The carriages were kept close by in the south range with its large arched openings and double doors. This range probably predates the others and was converted from a single-storey building. Underfloor heating was added in the mid-19th century to keep the family's two carriages – a Brougham and a Victoria – free of damp. The central door was later enlarged to accommodate a motor car.

The west range probably started as a small barn; it was later converted to stables and used in the 20th century to store the hound van. The northern end was also a stable, but was modified to house over 50 wet-cell batteries at the beginning of the 20th century. These were charged using electricity generated by a water wheel in the Rickyard and transferred to the house by overhead cables.

Walk past the stables back to the main drive. Turn right on the drive to leave Llanerchaeron

Top The Granary

Above The Heavy Horse Stable with the cowshed and bailiff's house beyond